Dedicated to my family.
Michael, Sienna, and Gabriel,
who are my earthly Saints.

Copyright © 2025 by Claudeen Martinez

All rights reserved.

No portion of this book may be reproduced in any form without written permission from the publisher or author, except as permitted by Australian copyright law.

Around the year 280, a baby named Nicholas was born in the busy town of Patara, in what is now Turkey. His parents were kind, generous, and loved God very much.

Nicholas was a gentle boy who loved to pray. He always looked for ways to help people. When he saw someone hungry, he shared his food. When he saw someone sad, he gave them a smile.

One day, Nicholas's mother and father became very sick and went to heaven. Nicholas was very sad, but he remembered how they had taught him to love and help others.

Nicholas heard about a family who had no money and no food. While they slept, he tiptoed to their house and left a little bag of gold for them, then ran away before anyone could see him!

Nicholas didn't stop there. He gave coins to the poor, clothes to those who were cold, and food to hungry families. He never said a word, he just smiled and disappeared

The people in the town began to wonder, 'Who is giving us these wonderful gifts?' They asked their neighbours and even looked for clues. But Nicholas never told anyone it was him.

As Nicholas grew older, he became a priest. He promised to love and care for the people just like Jesus did. He helped them pray, gave them advice, and shared God's love every day.

Because he was so wise and kind, the church made Nicholas a Bishop. He wore red robes and carried a gold staff, walking through the town with a smile, listening to people's needs.

Bishop Nicholas was brave. He helped children, protected the poor, and even calmed storms at sea when sailors were in danger. Everyone knew he was a man of courage and love.

Bishop Nicholas loved spending time in quiet prayer. He talked to Jesus in his heart and listened for Gods voice. Prayer gave him strength to keep helping others.

People who were sick or hurt would ask Nicholas to pray for them. And many times, after his prayer, they felt better. Gods love flowed through his kind hands.

When there was fighting or anger in a village, Bishop Nicholas would walk in and gently speak words of peace. He reminded everyone to forgive, to love, and to start again.

The whole town was filled with joy because of Bishop Nicholas. Children ran to see him, parents waved from their doors, and everyone felt happier when he was near.

Some people did not like that Nicholas loved Jesus. They locked him in jail, but he kept praying and trusting God. He knew that love and faith were stronger than fear.

Bishop Nicholas went to a big meeting called the Council of Nicaea. There, he helped others understand that Jesus is God's Son, full of love and truth, and he wants us to love each other too.

After many years of loving and serving others, Nicholas became very old. One quiet night, he whispered a prayer, closed his eyes, and peacefully went to heaven.

In heaven, the angels sang, and Jesus welcomed Nicholas with open arms. Heaven rejoiced because a life of love had returned home.

The people he had helped called him Saint Nicholas a holy friend of God. His love and kindness were never forgotten.

To remember him, people began celebrating Saint Nicholas's feast day on December 6th. On that day, children would wake up to find little surprises in their shoes.

After some time, the story of Saint Nicholas turned into the idea of Santa Claus, a jolly giver who brings gifts with love and cheer.

But Saint Nicholas isn't just about gifts and toys. He reminds us that real giving comes from the heart. Helping people is the best gift of all.

You don't need gold coins to be like Saint Nicholas. You can give a hug, a kind word, or help someone who needs a friend.

Sometimes the best gifts are given in secret when no one is looking, just like Saint Nicholas did.

Saint Nicholas loved children very much. He is a special friend to all kids, no matter where they live or what they have.

Every Christmas, we celebrate the birth of Jesus with joy and love. We remember Saint Nicholas by giving to others and being joyful.

You can talk to Saint Nicholas anytime. Ask him to help you be kind and joyful. He will pray for you and your family.

Saint Nicholas lived his life like a bright candle, shining in the darkness and lighting the way to Jesus. He showed us that helping and loving others lights up hearts around the world.

We thank you, Saint Nicholas, for your big heart, your prayers, and the way you remind us to care for others.

And guess what? You can be like Saint Nicholas too. When you give with joy, you become a light in the world!

The story of Saint Nicholas never really ends. Every time someone gives with love, his story grows brighter. Will you be a wonder worker too?

Dear Saint Nicholas,
You gave to others
with joy and love.
You shared what you had
and helped those in need.
Teach us to be generous, to give
without asking back, and to make
small sacrifices for the good of others.
Help us spread kindness
like you did every day.

www.ingramcontent.com/pod-product-compliance
Lightning Source LLC
Chambersburg PA
CBHW041507220426
43661CB00017B/1273